Special Thanks

Copywrite

This Fishing Journal belongs too:

Name:_____

Journal Number:_____

Start Date of Journal:_____

Fishing for Kids

Fishing is FUN! It gives you a great excuse to leave your computer, tablet or phone behind and venture out into the elements.

You can fish from a boat, a wharf or off the beach or rivers edge.

You can learn about fish names, but also about their shape and colors.

Choose your hook and line and learn the skill of patience

It's time to go fishing!

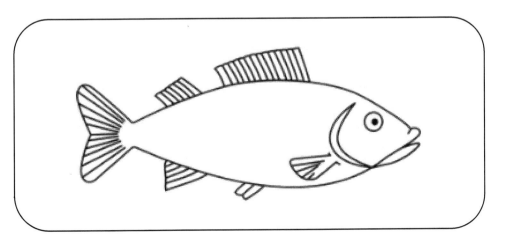

Fish Parts

Fish are amazing animals. We all dream about swimming through the water like a fast fish!

Below you can see all the parts that make up these amazing animals who can glide through the water with ease.

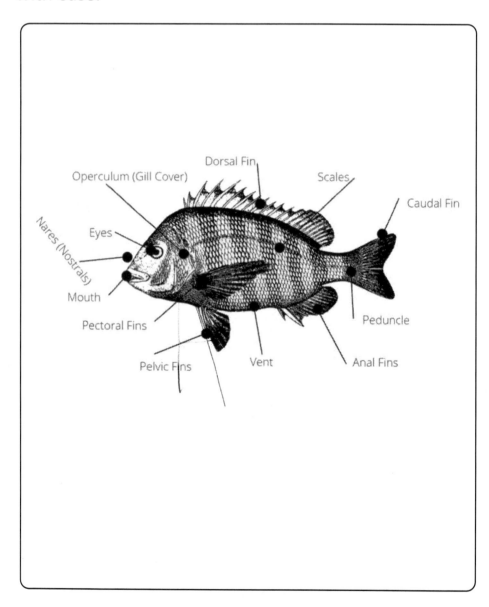

What you need to catch a Fish

Fishing is a great activity you can do with your family and friends. Its great to go with an Adult who can teach you how to fish, so you can get the excitement of catching your first fish.

Things you will need:
Fishing Rod and Reel
Fishing Line
Weights
Fish hooks
Bait, soft bait or fishing lures
Ask an Adult about a Fishing License (In some states)

Time to go Fishing!
Once you have all of the equipment you need then you can find many places to go fishing. It is important that you go with an Adult to ensure you are kept safe around water.

Catch and Release:
Make sure your fish you catch meets the legal or minimum size. If not, its important to quickly release it back into the water so that it can continue to grow to be caught again another day.

Leave only foot prints, take only photos
Make sure that you take all of your rubbish with you. Fishing hooks and lines can be dangerous to other wildlife such as birds, so its best you make sure you take it all with you when you finish your days fishing.

Fish Jokes

Q: What Kind of music should you listen to while fishing?
A: Something catchy!

Q: What does a fish do in a crisis?
A: They sea-kelp!

Q: What do you call a fish with one eye?
A: Fsssshhh!

Q: Which day do fish hate?
A: Fry-Day!

Q: How does a squid go into a fight?
A: Fully armed!

Q: What did the shark say after eating the clown fish?
A: That tasted a little funny!

Q: Why don't shellfish share?
A: Because they are shellfish!

Q: Where do fish sleep?
A: On the sea-bed!

Q: What do Giant Squids eat?
A: Fish and Ships!

Q: What do you call a fish that wont shut up?
A: A big-mouthed bass!

Q: How does a fish know how much it weights?
A: Because it has its own scales!

Q: How do you communicate with a fish?
A: You drop it a line!

Q: What do fish need to keep healthy?
A: Vitamin Sea!

FISHING LOG

SPECIES	WEIGHT	LENGTH	TIME	BAIT

FISHING JOURNAL

Fishing with _____

Date _____

Day of the week _____

Time _____

Location _____ GPS _____

Water

Salt Water ☐

Fresh Water ☐

Flat Water ☐

Waves ☐

Weather

Dry ☐

Wet ☐

Sunny ☐

Cloudy ☐

Fish Species _____

_____

Fish Length _____

Fish Weight _____

_____

How did you catch it? _____

_____

_____

Tell us about your day Fishing?

_____

_____

_____

Fish Sketch or Photograph

FISHING JOURNAL

Fishing with _____

Date _____

Day of the week _____

Time _____

Location _____ GPS _____

Water

Salt Water ☐

Fresh Water ☐

Flat Water ☐

Waves ☐

Weather

Dry ☐

Wet ☐

Sunny ☐

Cloudy ☐

Fish Species _____

_____

Fish Length _____

Fish Weight _____

_____

How did you catch it? _____

_____

_____

_____

Tell us about your day Fishing?

_____

_____

_____

Fish Sketch or Photograph

FISHING JOURNAL

Fishing with _____

Date _____

Day of the week _____

Time _____

Location _____ GPS _____

Water

Salt Water ☐

Fresh Water ☐

Flat Water ☐

Waves ☐

Weather

Dry ☐

Wet ☐

Sunny ☐

Cloudy ☐

Fish Species _____

_____

Fish Length _____

Fish Weight _____

_____

How did you catch it? _____

_____

_____

_____

Tell us about your day Fishing?

_____

_____

_____

Fish Sketch or Photograph

FISHING JOURNAL

Fishing with _____

Date _____

Day of the week _____

Time _____

Location _____ GPS _____

Water

Salt Water ☐

Fresh Water ☐

Flat Water ☐

Waves ☐

Weather

Dry ☐

Wet ☐

Sunny ☐

Cloudy ☐

Fish Species _____

_____

Fish Length _____

Fish Weight _____

_____

How did you catch it? _____

_____

_____

_____

Tell us about your day Fishing?

_____

_____

_____

Fish Sketch or Photograph

FISHING JOURNAL

Fishing with _____

Date _____

Day of the week _____

Time _____

Location _____ GPS _____

Water

Salt Water ☐

Fresh Water ☐

Flat Water ☐

Waves ☐

Weather

Dry ☐

Wet ☐

Sunny ☐

Cloudy ☐

Fish Species _____

_____

Fish Length _____

Fish Weight _____

_____

How did you catch it? _____

_____

_____

_____

Tell us about your day Fishing?

_____

_____

_____

Fish Sketch or Photograph

FISHING LOG

SPECIES	WEIGHT	LENGTH	TIME	BAIT

FISHING JOURNAL

Fishing with _____
Date _____
Day of the week _____
Time _____
Location _____ GPS _____

Water		**Weather**	
Salt Water	☐	Dry	☐
Fresh Water	☐	Wet	☐
Flat Water	☐	Sunny	☐
Waves	☐	Cloudy	☐

Fish Species _____

_____

Fish Length _____

Fish Weight _____

_____

How did you catch it? _____

_____

_____

_____

Tell us about your day Fishing?

_____

_____

_____

Fish Sketch or Photograph

FISHING JOURNAL

Fishing with _____

Date _____

Day of the week _____

Time _____

Location _____ GPS _____

Water

Salt Water ☐

Fresh Water ☐

Flat Water ☐

Waves ☐

Weather

Dry ☐

Wet ☐

Sunny ☐

Cloudy ☐

Fish Species _____

_____

Fish Length _____

Fish Weight _____

_____

How did you catch it? _____

_____

_____

_____

Tell us about your day Fishing?

Fish Sketch or Photograph

FISHING JOURNAL

Fishing with _____

Date _____

Day of the week _____

Time _____

Location _____ GPS _____

Water

Salt Water ☐

Fresh Water ☐

Flat Water ☐

Waves ☐

Weather

Dry ☐

Wet ☐

Sunny ☐

Cloudy ☐

Fish Species _____

_____

Fish Length _____

Fish Weight _____

_____

How did you catch it? _____

_____

_____

_____

Tell us about your day Fishing?

_____

_____

_____

Fish Sketch or Photograph

FISHING JOURNAL

Fishing with _____
Date _____
Day of the week _____
Time _____
Location _____ GPS _____

Water

Salt Water ☐
Fresh Water ☐
Flat Water ☐
Waves ☐

Weather

Dry ☐
Wet ☐
Sunny ☐
Cloudy ☐

Fish Species _____
_____

Fish Length _____
Fish Weight _____
_____

How did you catch it? _____
_____
_____
_____

Tell us about your day Fishing?

_____

_____

_____

Fish Sketch or Photograph

FISHING JOURNAL

Fishing with _____

Date _____

Day of the week _____

Time _____

Location _____ GPS _____

Water

Salt Water ☐

Fresh Water ☐

Flat Water ☐

Waves ☐

Weather

Dry ☐

Wet ☐

Sunny ☐

Cloudy ☐

Fish Species _____

_____

Fish Length _____

Fish Weight _____

_____

How did you catch it? _____

_____

_____

_____

Tell us about your day Fishing?

_____

_____

_____

Fish Sketch or Photograph

FISHING LOG

SPECIES	WEIGHT	LENGTH	TIME	BAIT

FISHING JOURNAL

Fishing with _____

Date _____

Day of the week _____

Time _____

Location _____ GPS _____

Water

Salt Water ☐

Fresh Water ☐

Flat Water ☐

Waves ☐

Weather

Dry ☐

Wet ☐

Sunny ☐

Cloudy ☐

Fish Species _____

_____

Fish Length _____

Fish Weight _____

_____

How did you catch it? _____

_____

_____

_____

Tell us about your day Fishing?

_____

_____

_____

Fish Sketch or Photograph

FISHING JOURNAL

Fishing with _____

Date _____

Day of the week _____

Time _____

Location _____ GPS _____

Water

Salt Water ☐

Fresh Water ☐

Flat Water ☐

Waves ☐

Weather

Dry ☐

Wet ☐

Sunny ☐

Cloudy ☐

Fish Species _____

_____

Fish Length _____

Fish Weight _____

_____

How did you catch it? _____

_____

_____

_____

Tell us about your day Fishing?

_____

_____

_____

Fish Sketch or Photograph

FISHING JOURNAL

Fishing with _____

Date _____

Day of the week _____

Time _____

Location _____ GPS _____

Water
Salt Water ☐

Fresh Water ☐

Flat Water ☐

Waves ☐

Weather
Dry ☐

Wet ☐

Sunny ☐

Cloudy ☐

Fish Species _____

_____

Fish Length _____

Fish Weight _____

_____

How did you catch it? _____

_____

_____

_____

Tell us about your day Fishing?

_____

_____

_____

Fish Sketch or Photograph

FISHING JOURNAL

Fishing with _____

Date _____

Day of the week _____

Time _____

Location _____ GPS _____

Water

Salt Water ☐

Fresh Water ☐

Flat Water ☐

Waves ☐

Weather

Dry ☐

Wet ☐

Sunny ☐

Cloudy ☐

Fish Species _____

_____

Fish Length _____

Fish Weight _____

_____

How did you catch it? _____

_____

_____

_____

Tell us about your day Fishing?

_____

_____

_____

Fish Sketch or Photograph

FISHING JOURNAL

Fishing with _____

Date _____

Day of the week _____

Time _____

Location _____ GPS _____

Water

Salt Water ☐

Fresh Water ☐

Flat Water ☐

Waves ☐

Weather

Dry ☐

Wet ☐

Sunny ☐

Cloudy ☐

Fish Species _____

_____

Fish Length _____

Fish Weight _____

_____

How did you catch it? _____

_____

_____

_____

Tell us about your day Fishing?

_____

_____

_____

Fish Sketch or Photograph

FISHING LOG

SPECIES	WEIGHT	LENGTH	TIME	BAIT

FISHING JOURNAL

Fishing with _____

Date _____

Day of the week _____

Time _____

Location _____ GPS _____

Water

Salt Water ☐

Fresh Water ☐

Flat Water ☐

Waves ☐

Weather

Dry ☐

Wet ☐

Sunny ☐

Cloudy ☐

Fish Species _____

_____

Fish Length _____

Fish Weight _____

_____

How did you catch it? _____

_____

_____

_____

Tell us about your day Fishing?

_____

_____

_____

Fish Sketch or Photograph

FISHING JOURNAL

Fishing with _____

Date _____

Day of the week _____

Time _____

Location _____ GPS _____

Water

Salt Water ☐

Fresh Water ☐

Flat Water ☐

Waves ☐

Weather

Dry ☐

Wet ☐

Sunny ☐

Cloudy ☐

Fish Species _____

_____

Fish Length _____

Fish Weight _____

_____

How did you catch it? _____

_____

_____

_____

Tell us about your day Fishing?

_____

_____

_____

Fish Sketch or Photograph

FISHING JOURNAL

Fishing with _____

Date _____

Day of the week _____

Time _____

Location _____ GPS _____

Water

Salt Water ☐

Fresh Water ☐

Flat Water ☐

Waves ☐

Weather

Dry ☐

Wet ☐

Sunny ☐

Cloudy ☐

Fish Species _____

_____

Fish Length _____

Fish Weight _____

_____

How did you catch it? _____

_____

_____

_____

Tell us about your day Fishing?

_____

_____

_____

Fish Sketch or Photograph

FISHING JOURNAL

Fishing with _____
Date _____
Day of the week _____
Time _____
Location _____ GPS _____

Water

Salt Water ☐

Fresh Water ☐

Flat Water ☐

Waves ☐

Weather

Dry ☐

Wet ☐

Sunny ☐

Cloudy ☐

Fish Species _____
_____

Fish Length _____

Fish Weight _____
_____

How did you catch it? _____
_____
_____
_____

Tell us about your day Fishing?

_____

_____

_____

Fish Sketch or Photograph

FISHING JOURNAL

Fishing with _____

Date _____

Day of the week _____

Time _____

Location _____ GPS _____

Water

Salt Water ☐

Fresh Water ☐

Flat Water ☐

Waves ☐

Weather

Dry ☐

Wet ☐

Sunny ☐

Cloudy ☐

Fish Species _____

_____

Fish Length _____

Fish Weight _____

_____

How did you catch it? _____

_____

_____

_____

Tell us about your day Fishing?

_____

_____

_____

Fish Sketch or Photograph

FISHING LOG

SPECIES	WEIGHT	LENGTH	TIME	BAIT

FISHING JOURNAL

Fishing with _____

Date _____

Day of the week _____

Time _____

Location _____ GPS _____

Water

Salt Water ☐

Fresh Water ☐

Flat Water ☐

Waves ☐

Weather

Dry ☐

Wet ☐

Sunny ☐

Cloudy ☐

Fish Species _____

_____

Fish Length _____

Fish Weight _____

_____

How did you catch it? _____

_____

_____

_____

Tell us about your day Fishing?

_____

_____

_____

Fish Sketch or Photograph

FISHING JOURNAL

Fishing with _____

Date _____

Day of the week _____

Time _____

Location _____ GPS _____

Water

Salt Water ☐

Fresh Water ☐

Flat Water ☐

Waves ☐

Weather

Dry ☐

Wet ☐

Sunny ☐

Cloudy ☐

Fish Species _____

_____

Fish Length _____

Fish Weight _____

_____

How did you catch it? _____

_____

_____

_____

Tell us about your day Fishing?

_____

_____

_____

Fish Sketch or Photograph

FISHING JOURNAL

Fishing with _____

Date _____

Day of the week _____

Time _____

Location _____ GPS _____

Water

Salt Water ☐

Fresh Water ☐

Flat Water ☐

Waves ☐

Weather

Dry ☐

Wet ☐

Sunny ☐

Cloudy ☐

Fish Species _____

_____

Fish Length _____

Fish Weight _____

_____

How did you catch it? _____

_____

_____

_____

Tell us about your day Fishing?

_____

_____

_____

Fish Sketch or Photograph

FISHING JOURNAL

Fishing with _____

Date _____

Day of the week _____

Time _____

Location _____ GPS _____

Water

Salt Water ☐

Fresh Water ☐

Flat Water ☐

Waves ☐

Weather

Dry ☐

Wet ☐

Sunny ☐

Cloudy ☐

Fish Species _____

Fish Length _____

Fish Weight _____

How did you catch it? _____

_____

_____

Tell us about your day Fishing?

_____

_____

_____

Fish Sketch or Photograph

FISHING JOURNAL

Fishing with _____

Date _____

Day of the week _____

Time _____

Location _____ GPS _____

Water

Salt Water ☐

Fresh Water ☐

Flat Water ☐

Waves ☐

Weather

Dry ☐

Wet ☐

Sunny ☐

Cloudy ☐

Fish Species _____

_____

Fish Length _____

Fish Weight _____

_____

How did you catch it? _____

_____

_____

_____

Tell us about your day Fishing?

_____

_____

_____

Fish Sketch or Photograph

FISHING LOG

SPECIES	WEIGHT	LENGTH	TIME	BAIT

FISHING JOURNAL

Fishing with _____

Date _____

Day of the week _____

Time _____

Location _____ GPS _____

Water

Salt Water ☐

Fresh Water ☐

Flat Water ☐

Waves ☐

Weather

Dry ☐

Wet ☐

Sunny ☐

Cloudy ☐

Fish Species _____

_____

Fish Length _____

Fish Weight _____

_____

How did you catch it? _____

_____

_____

_____

Tell us about your day Fishing?

_____

_____

_____

Fish Sketch or Photograph

FISHING JOURNAL

Fishing with _____

Date _____

Day of the week _____

Time _____

Location _____ GPS _____

Water

Salt Water ☐

Fresh Water ☐

Flat Water ☐

Waves ☐

Weather

Dry ☐

Wet ☐

Sunny ☐

Cloudy ☐

Fish Species _____

_____

Fish Length _____

Fish Weight _____

_____

How did you catch it? _____

_____

_____

_____

Tell us about your day Fishing?

_____

_____

_____

Fish Sketch or Photograph

FISHING JOURNAL

Fishing with _____

Date _____

Day of the week _____

Time _____

Location _____ GPS _____

Water

Salt Water ☐

Fresh Water ☐

Flat Water ☐

Waves ☐

Weather

Dry ☐

Wet ☐

Sunny ☐

Cloudy ☐

Fish Species _____

_____

Fish Length _____

Fish Weight _____

_____

How did you catch it? _____

_____

_____

_____

Tell us about your day Fishing?

_____

_____

_____

Fish Sketch or Photograph

FISHING JOURNAL

Fishing with _____

Date _____

Day of the week _____

Time _____

Location _____ GPS _____

Water

Salt Water ☐

Fresh Water ☐

Flat Water ☐

Waves ☐

Weather

Dry ☐

Wet ☐

Sunny ☐

Cloudy ☐

Fish Species _____

_____

Fish Length _____

Fish Weight _____

_____

How did you catch it? _____

_____

_____

_____

Tell us about your day Fishing?

_____

_____

_____

Fish Sketch or Photograph

FISHING JOURNAL

Fishing with _____

Date _____

Day of the week _____

Time _____

Location _____ GPS _____

Water

Salt Water ☐

Fresh Water ☐

Flat Water ☐

Waves ☐

Weather

Dry ☐

Wet ☐

Sunny ☐

Cloudy ☐

Fish Species _____

_____

Fish Length _____

Fish Weight _____

_____

How did you catch it? _____

_____

_____

_____

Tell us about your day Fishing?

_____

_____

_____

Fish Sketch or Photograph

Made in the USA
Middletown, DE
27 May 2020